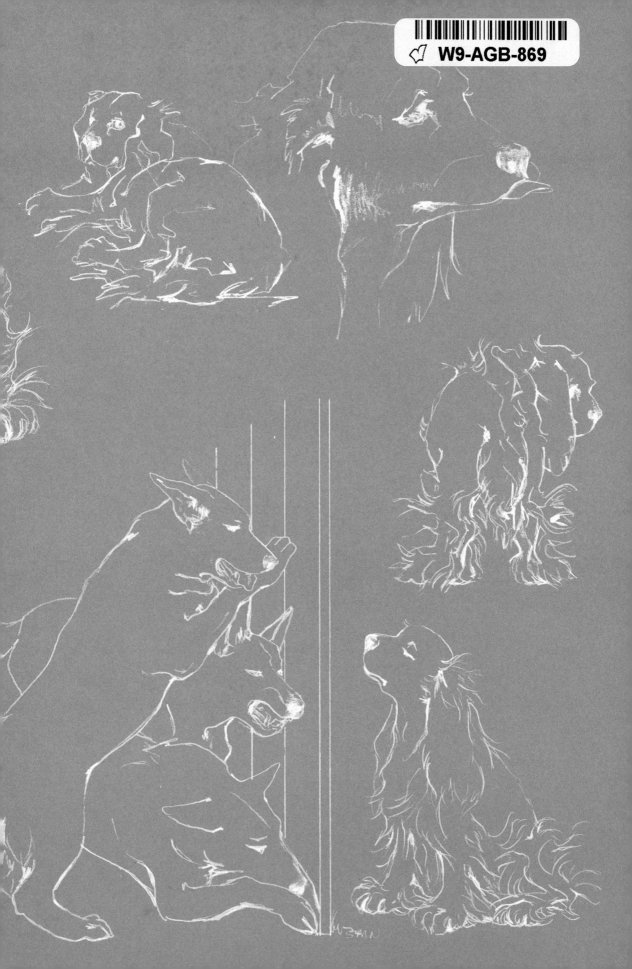

C. FRED'S STORY

C. Fred's Story

C. Fred Bush

Edited slightly by Barbara Bush

Doubleday & Company, Inc., Garden City, New York   1984

PICTURE CREDITS

Torie Clark (Frontispiece)

Cynthia Johnson 3, 5, 7, 9, 20, 30, 36, 45, 47, 53, 55, 56, 57, 60, 63, 66, 69, 73, 81, 82, 84, 87, 90, 94, 96, 97, 98, 99, 101, 103, 104, 106, 107, 108

David Bray 15, 41

Barbara Bush 19, 48, 70, 77

Marvin Bush 29

Valerie Hodgson 59, 65, 105

Judith Chiles 88

Lydia Heston 95

John Fisher Burns 17

Dean Lee 100

Library of Congress Cataloging in Publication Data

Bush, Barbara, 1925–
    C. Fred's story.

    1. Bush, George, 1924–   —Anecdotes. 2. Dogs—Anecdotes. I. Title.
E840.8.B87B87 1984   973.927'092'4
ISBN: 0-385-18971-0
Library of Congress Card Catalog Number 83–14074
Copyright © 1984 by Barbara Bush

Bar and I want to thank the following very special people for their most generous contributions to *C. Fred's Story:* Cynthia Johnson, Valerie Hodgson, David Bray and various members of our family for *donating* their pictures to this book.

We want to thank Jane Kenny for typing the final manuscript. (In spite of any and all photos of me at the keyboards, I don't type.) We would also like to thank our editor, Lisa Drew, for encouraging us. Lastly, we want to thank Sally Neblett for her very talented sketches of me.

All the above gave their time and skills gladly and made the writing of this book a joy. To them so many *thanks!*

My part of the dedication goes to Marvin Bush, who rescued me from the store; Paula Rendon, who loves me and cares for me; and Don Rhodes, who is my very best friend in the whole wide world.

C.F.B.

My part of the dedication goes to George Bush, whose fascinating career has made this story possible and because he is my very best friend in the whole wide world.

B.P.B.

Contents

C . FRED'S STORY

In the Beginning

I was born in Kansas City in 1973. Thank heavens, I was born on April 2 and not a day earlier. My mother's name was Judy and my father's name was Tex.

Of course C. Fred doesn't remember his mother or father. He was only eight weeks old when he was weaned and sent off to a Pup Fair store.

I am a cocker spaniel. There is definitely some discussion about my color. Pup Fair says I am a blond. One thing you may be sure of is that I am a boy.

When I was eight weeks old I had a miserable time being shipped in a cage to Washington, D.C. There I joined many other dogs and people came and looked at us. I wouldn't treat a person like that.

Translated: I wouldn't treat a dog like that.

Very soon after I arrived two men came into the pet shop. One was a big boy with curly hair named Marvin Bush. He looked deeply into my eyes and immediately said, "Yep, *this* is the dog we want!" I later learned that Marvin and Don Rhodes had been to many stores and seen many pups. Don had urged Marvin to take any number of other dogs, but Marvin turned them all down. I was to be a birthday present for his mother and he wanted just the right dog. So Marvin became my first friend and although it took years, Don became my very best friend. I am a people dog. That is, I have always lived with people in their homes. I have never been in a doghouse.

1

Maybe not in a doghouse, C. Fred, but several times in the doghouse.

That night the family was sitting around trying to decide what I was to be named. Marvin and Bar (his mother, the birthday girl) threw out names like "Josh," "Chris" and other names that they considered good, strong dog names, when George, the father, said, "Not at all. We Bushes have always named our children after people we loved." So they thought and thought and came up with the catchy name of "C. Fred Bush." I am named after George's best friend, C. Fred Chambers of Houston, Texas. I have met him many times and he doesn't really seem to appreciate the great honor that the Bushes bestowed upon him. Often he and his wife Marion say that they are going to call their dogs George and Bar, but they haven't so far.

My official American Kennel Club name is C. Fred's Tex, after my dog father and my adopted state. The A.K.C. says that I am buff-colored.

Some people call me "Siegfried." Others call me "See Fred," as in "See Fred run." Mr. Justice Stewart calls me "J. Fred." My name is Charles Frederick Bush, C. Fred for short.

I have never dared tell C. Fred that J. Fred Muggs was a chimpanzee.

Aren't people funny? George and Bar raved to Marvin about his thoughtful, wonderful gift and then I overheard them talking that first night. "Gosh, I really wanted to pick out my own dog." "Cocker spaniels are too high-strung." "They get fat and are stupid." "I had a friend who had one once and had to get rid of it, as it yapped all the time." And on and on.

I am sorry that Freddy heard that. We said it and much more.

So I had to work a little harder. I smiled a lot and never cried at night.

Sure, after we put him on our bed.

I tried to look smart and must have succeeded, for there are those who think that I look like Walter Cronkite . . . at times.

True, it has been said.

I have certainly kept my figure.

Right.

I didn't yap for the first two years.

Sure, but how about the next seven?

George worked for the Republican National Committee; in fact, he was the chairman of the committee when I went to live with the Bushes. He traveled all the time. Bar and I only traveled with him to Kennebunkport, Maine. In Maine, Bar put me in a bag and carried me to the tennis club on her moped. There I waited while she played tennis. Often we went boating with George. We fished for bluefish and mackerel. When this happened I was happy. People don't eat pollack but sea gulls do and I love watching them try to fly after they swallow a whole pollack. Sometimes at low tide George takes us to Gull Island and we watch the seals play and swim. At times I get seasick. I don't always feel like going in the boat, but I love being with people. I'd rather suffer a little than be left home alone.

I swam a lot in Maine. I love the salt water. We went over to Walker's Point and I swam in Uncle Herbie's pool. No other dogs did this.

You bet they didn't. This was not C. Fred's finest hour. Years later when we moved to Walker's Point, C. Fred swam legitimately.

During my years of summers in Maine I jogged with Bar and George. I learned to run on a leash next to Bar's moped.

Only after my children told me it embarrassed them to see me riding with C. Fred in a sling bag over my shoulder and my tennis racquet on my back.

I also learned to fish and stay clear of hooks and I chased raccoons, cats and skunks. I can hardly tell them apart.

That's for sure. The score is skunk three, C. Fred zero.

I love Maine. We even went in the winter the year I was eight. We were there for Thanksgiving and Easter. I loved it! We played in the snow and Bar and I went cross-country skiing. I didn't like it when snow got caught between my toes. I could hardly walk.

Back in Washington, that first year, Bar taught me how to sit up, roll over, catch biscuits, walk like a man—in fact, a whole bag of tricks. Speaking of tricks, George spent that whole year fighting a whole bag of "Dirty Tricks" that had taken place the year before.

Come on, Freddy, we agreed—no politics.

I did have two dog friends, Amos Stewart and Tasha Moore. Amos belongs to Bar's great friend, Andy Stewart (one of my favorite ladies, too), and Tasha belongs to wonderful neighbors, Tabb and Rosie Moore. Amos and I have remained friends throughout the years. Amos and Tasha are great big dogs. We three constantly knocked over garbage cans and ate garbage. Many people hated us in the neighborhood and Rosie Moore, Andy Stewart and Barbara Bush hated picking up other people's garbage.

Right.

Amos went off to "camp" sometimes. I later discovered that he really went to a "fat farm." Although he and Andy much preferred that we all said "camp." Andy says Amos is a thoroughbred—she says he is a thoroughbred German shepherd and a thoroughbred Border collie. That's a thoroughbred?

A China Dog

In the summer of 1974 Barbara was living in our gray house in Maine for the month of August. All the children were coming to visit us and George came for weekends. I could tell George was worried. One day Barbara got a phone call from George, who was in California, saying, "Why not meet me in D.C. tomorrow. Something's come up. I'm cutting my trip short and you ought to be with me." Something certainly did happen! The United States President resigned and our whole life changed. Bar left for Washington and when she came back George was with her. They gathered the children together and had them guess what job was next for George. Nobody guessed. Although nobody was more interested than I, I wasn't consulted. They kept talking about Peking and nobody mentioned me ever, not even once.

Oh yes we did, and each time George said, "He can't go. They don't like dogs in China."

We returned to Washington and one day Bar whispered to me, "Good news, Freddy. They have lots of diplomatic dogs in Peking." So she bought seventeen cases of dog food and sent them off to China with their other goods.

At the time this seemed the only way to get George to agree. The investment in dog food was so big that we just couldn't afford not to take C. Fred with us. Incidentally, it was easier to get Freddy into China than any of our children or houseguests.

13

Nobody prepared me for the trip to China. I, who slept with chairmen and chiefs, was put in a cage where I stayed for four days. I spent three of these days in quarantine in Japan while Barbara and George were having a glorious visit with the ambassador and his wife. Maybe this was to prepare me for what was to come later. There was certainly no freedom in China for me. I landed and was brought with the luggage to the United States Liaison Office. With the baggage! A man brought me to the house and opened the door of the cage. I heard Bar's voice, flew up the stairs, leapt into her arms and lathered her with kisses.

And that's not all. My darling Freddy had a slight accident.

I quickly found the perimeter of our property and where I could go and where I couldn't go. The latter was immense—all of China. The former was the walled compound where we had our house in one building and George's office in another. Between the two buildings was a fenced-in yard where I spent my days eating a bone or playing with a ball. I growled if someone came near my bone.

Did he ever! George and I try to never get between C. Fred and a bone. He is such a grump.

Some days when Bar was away and it was really cold outside, George let me go into the office. Everyone was nice to me; especially the United States security guards. They let me go on the rounds with them.

14

Outside of our compound gate stood two guards, members of the People's Liberation Army. For fourteen months I tried in vain to get them to look at me.

Inside the house there were some Chinese people to help us: a Mr. Sung and his helper, a Mrs. Chien, a Mrs. Wang, a Mr. Wang and a Mr. Chien.

That may seem confusing. In China there are only about two hundred surnames. Many people have the same names. These Wangs and Chiens were not related.

I teased Mrs. Chien and Mrs. Wang just like I teased Paula at home. I often stole their dustcloths and made them chase me. At first they were afraid of me and Bar was afraid that I was going to cause an international incident. In fact, all the Chinese were afraid of me at first, so each time new people came to work in the house, Bar would have me do all my tricks. When nobody was around, the Chinese patted me. I liked them. Needless to say, when George had official Chinese come to visit, I was banished to an upstairs bedroom. One of my favorite Chinese friends was Mrs. Tang, George and Bar's Chinese teacher. She came every day at noon and taught them nice things to say in Chinese. I always sat in on the lessons.

In 1952 the Chinese had systematically searched out and killed all dogs. They were scavengers and thieves, roaming the streets in packs, sick with rabies. So the Chinese, who had loved dogs in the "bad old days," were taught that dogs were dangerous, dirty and, a bigger threat, they ate food that the starving population needed.

Every morning when we lived in China, Bar or George walked me around the compound before breakfast. Sometimes I tried to make a break for the street to chase a wagon drawn by two donkeys and a skinny little horse or some other such interesting vehicle. I was always caught and brought back.

George and Bar explored Peking on their bikes. I was so jealous and wished I was back in Maine. Sometimes Bar put a long rope on my harness and rode up and down the street with me by her side. She didn't stay out too long because the crowds gathered.

Bar hit tennis balls to me in the driveway, being careful to keep the balls inside the compound. George, on the other hand, hit balls to me in the driveway, being careful to hit them outside the compound into the street to attract the schoolchildren walking back to school. Bar had me do my tricks so the children could see me. Without warning she stopped doing this and I missed seeing the children peek in the gate.

The People's Liberation Army guards scolded the children and made them move on. So of course I stopped encouraging them, as I didn't want to cause them any pain.

I had more baths in China. Bar says that I am honey-colored, but in China I was a gray. The pollution was so bad you could see the gray climbing up my legs and in twenty-four hours I was gray again.

As previously mentioned, we did sleep with Fred at our feet and therefore a clean C. Fred was much to be desired, especially as he inched up toward the pillow as the night drew on.

One day in May of 1975 the Chinese announced that there would be no more hot water for three weeks. It was annual clean-the-hot-water-pipes-spring-cleaning-time. They heat the water centrally in China, which means it is heated in a centrally located place downtown. No more baths for me for three weeks while the Chinese blew the dirt from the pipes. I went from gray to grayer.

Not only is the water heated centrally in Peking, but so are the houses. All the heat comes from burning coal and charcoal, thus the pollution.

I met several dogs in China, including a large black Canadian poodle and a funny little terrier named Bubbles, who belonged to an American married to a German reporter. Bar liked Bubbles's family very much. I did not like Bubbles at all. I missed Amos.

We had lots of houseguests and Bar put a sign in their rooms.

Beware of the Bush Dragon. He eats socks, furs, gloves and slippers. Please keep your doors closed or put your things up high. His name is C. Fred.

This was a great challenge to me and there were very few guests who escaped. I especially liked one guest who wore cashmere socks. He told Bar that I could unpack locked suitcases. But my very favorite was Mrs. Hamon from Dallas, Texas. The day they were leaving she left her fur coat and hat on her bed and went to have a last cup of coffee with George. The coat was too big, but the hat was just right. I had a nice chew and then pranced into the living room to show one and all. Usually I have trouble getting anyone to chase and play with me. This time Mr. and Mrs. Hamon joined in the game. I was in heaven, all four adults playing with me at one time. I liked Mrs. Hamon. She brushed up the fur and claimed that the hole that was there, wasn't.

It was touch and go for Fred that day and he does owe Mrs. Hamon a big thank-you.

Once when George took Barbara on a trip Jennifer Fitzgerald dog-sat with me. I moved right into her apartment. One night Jennifer was having a date. She rushed me home, gave me dinner and then ran in to bathe and change for her evening out. As she and her date were just relaxing with a drink, I thought a little game would be fun and came prancing into the living room with her panty hose hanging out of my mouth. This was greeted by a deep silence and there was no chase. Jennifer laughed. I liked Jennifer.

Jennifer also took me to the Great Wall of China, started in 500 B.C. and completed around 221 B.C. This wall meanders some fifteen hundred miles across the northern part of China. Bar and George didn't dare let me walk on the wall. Jennifer did, but even she winced when I performed on the Great Wall of China. I don't know why. After all, it was outdoors. Sometimes I don't understand people.

On the way home from the Great Wall we always stopped for a picnic lunch at the Ming tombs. The approach to the Ming tombs was guarded by the famous Avenue of the Animals, twelve stone animals on each side, twenty-four in all. Some of these seated and standing animals were real and some were mythical. Our guests always wanted to stop for pictures. Bar often put me on a rope and walked ahead with me up this marvelous sacred way, past the stone animals, the stone human statues and through gigantic red gates. All the time the commune members eyed me with great interest.

The Chinese do have dogs in the country, but all these dogs run to a hound look. All "sleeve" dogs were killed because they represented decadence and the bad old days. A "sleeve" dog was a dog who fitted into a mandarin sleeve like a Pekingese, a Lhasa apso or a Shih Tzu.

I loved the Ming tombs. This was the only place I could really run free. There are thirteen tombs about one half mile apart in a lovely valley. There are two big tourist tombs: the excavated tomb of Wan Li, the Porcelain Emperor, and the tomb of Yong Le, the second Ming Emperor. I couldn't go there because the Chinese didn't like dogs, and after being surrounded daily by a fourth of the world's population, I didn't like people!

It was to those tombs that the Chinese and their foreign tourist friends went because that's where the buses went. No Chinese own their own cars. Every car in China is owned by the government with the exception of the diplomats' cars. Diplomats needed permission to travel anywhere outside the twenty-mile limit except the Great Wall and the Ming tombs.

My favorite tomb was the De Ling, the tomb of the Carpenter Emperor, T'ien Ch'i, who was very minor. This was a crumbly old tomb surrounded by a faded red wall topped with green and gold tiles. It was peaceful and quiet and Bar and guests ate on the old altar under several-hundred-year-old white pines and other evergreens while I ran and sniffed, begged food and chased imaginary dragons and phoenixes over broken altar pieces, cracked tiles, shards and through the tall grasses. Once when we arrived at the De Ling we found a herd of goats eating away and we retreated to another tomb that day. Bar and the houseguests explored the tomb, looked at the stele that rose out of the turtle's back and talked of times past while I ran and explored.

I remember the day well. That was the first day that I realized that we were being observed. No sooner had we arrived than a man on a motorbike appeared, and it suddenly occurred to me that I had seen him on each visit. I came to look for him and he never failed me.

As I implied earlier, we had wall-to-wall houseguests and we also had three visits from Dr. Henry Kissinger and one from President Ford. I was excluded from the Ford visit, but I was very much included in the first Kissinger visit. Dr. Kissinger, his wife, Nancy, and two children came for Thanksgiving lunch in 1974. It was a very quiet time, just family. I was invited in and Dr. Kissinger allowed as how he liked me. I liked him because he fed me candied Chinese nuts, one for him and one for me. I later heard George teasing Bar: "How come you let Henry feed Fred between meals when you won't let me?"

Andy came to visit once, but without Amos!

Every evening, no matter what the time or weather, Bar took me for a walk outside the gates before bedtime. We took a twenty-minute walk. Often a houseguest would come with us. George could rarely be persuaded to come with us, as he really only enjoys active competitive sports. We walked in the dark streets with the almost silent swishing of some of the four million bicycles in Peking going by, taking people to and from work. We took the same walk every night, past the Temple of the Sun Park, by the embassies—the British, the North Vietnamese, the Egyptian, the Rumanian, the Cuban and the Polish. I chased the Polish cat every night. I was on a long, long rope and never caught him.

One day George had been persuaded to take a walk with us. Suddenly he realized that people were looking at me with wonder in their eyes. He said in Chinese, *"Ta shi shau go* [He's a little dog]." Then all the Chinese said, "Oh, he's a little dog. He's not a cat." Not a cat! What a blow. Frankly I had thought that the Chinese connected me in someway with their great hero Chairman Mao. I often noticed that they said *mao* when they saw me. It turned out that *mao* said one way means "Chairman Mao" and another means "cat," my bitterest enemy!

Many young Chinese had never seen a curly, long-haired dog. In his early days Freddy was more of a hippy type. Most people thought him quite feminine and would say, "Isn't she pretty?" For heaven's sake, don't tell C. Fred.

Bar learned to greet the Chinese with *"Ni bu pa. Ta shi shau go. Ta bu yau ren.* [Don't be afraid. He's a little dog. He doesn't bite people]." We made more friends.

I loved going for walks with George. He always gave me more rope and even let me off to chase the Polish cat. When George got to the last corner before our compound gate he would let me off the leash and we'd race to the house. One night when I was walking alone with Bar, we got to the corner and she let me off the leash. I raced away, but not to our house. I raced right across the street, past the PLA guards, up the steps and into the embassy of our neighbors from Gabon. This is how I went to my first dance. The chargé from Gabon was having an African dance and the music was too much for me to resist. Bar charged in after me and had to march the length of the dance floor to where I stood laughing at the end of the ballroom.

Absolutely right. He was laughing and I could have killed him.

中 华 人 民 共 和 国
北 京 动 物 检 疫 站
(PEKING ANIMAL QUARANTINE SERVICE,
THE PEOPLE'S REPUBLIC OF CHINA)

地址： 北京市西城区冰窖口胡同75号
(ADDRESS: 75 Ping-chiao-kou Lane,
Western District Peking.)

检 疫 证 书
(QUARANTINE CERTIFICATE)

第　　77　　号
(No.　　　　　)

1975 年 11 月 26 日
(DATE Nov 26th 1975)

发 货 人 ：
(Consignor:)

美 国 驻 中 国 联 络 处
(The American Liaison Office, Peking
of China)

受 货 人 ：
(Consignee:)

布 什
(Mr. Bush)

发 货 日 期 ：
(Date of Despatch:)

1975年12月7日
(Dec 7th 1975)

到 达 地 点 ：
(Place of Destination:)

波 士 顿 华 盛 顿
(Boston, washington)

动物种类和数量等：
(Kind and quantity
of Animal etc:)

一只 3 岁黄色公狗
(Only one dog, 3 years, yellow, Male.)

鉴 定 ：
(Opinion:)

健 康
(Healthy)

一 个 月 有 效
(Valid for one month)

站 长
(Director)

检 疫 员
(Quarantine Inspector)

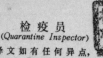

本证书译文如有任何异点，概以中文为主。
(N. B. In case of divergence, the Chinese text shall be regarded as authentic.)

Bar and George went to the Fur Fair and came home and said, "Some good news and some bad news, Freddy. The good news is that we saw a beautiful coat made of cat." Before I had time to enjoy this amusing tidbit, they told me the bad news. They had also seen a blond coat made of dog fur. So I, with my beautiful buff, blond, honey-colored coat, always felt just a little threatened after that.

Shortly before we were to leave China the Chinese officials served dog at the Great Hall of the People and our Arab friends were insulted because they think dog is dirty. So what's with people? They wear dog, eat dog and think it's dirty?

Another time George came home from a banquet and could hardly meet my eye. He had been served and had eaten "upper lip of wild dog," after which he'd been told what it was. From then on until we left I could never tell if the Chinese liked me for me alone or as a potential coat or little dog stew. So in December of 1975 when we left, I left with some regret and much relief!

Poor C. Fred almost didn't get his papers and permit to leave China. But George intervened and Fred's papers were signed. He was referred to as "only one yellow dog." Call him what you will, blond, honey-colored, buff, gray or yellow. He's out of China.

CIA Year

On the return from China, George became the director of the Central Intelligence Agency. George found this job more interesting than any he had ever held before. He respected and liked the people, and he was impressed with their dedication and wisdom. The following is what Bar and I knew about George's job:

George told us nothing. He said Bar and I couldn't keep a secret, therefore he didn't tell us any. He was right about Bar. Her favorite sentence starts "Don't tell George I told you, but . . ." He was wrong about me. Later I met another director of the Central Intelligence Agency, William Casey, and had an opportunity to tell him a lot of secrets.

I quickly took up my old ways, walking with Amos and Andy, dumping over garbage cans and guarding our tiny yard.

It was during this period that a big champagne-colored poodle came into our lives. He looked very sweet and he led an elderly man up and down our street on a leash. We felt this was outrageous. This was our own tiny dead-end street and this dog was trespassing. Whenever he passed us he called Amos and me "wimps, cowards and sissies." He tried hard to pick a fight and when we did fight him, he whined to his master and his master whined back.

You bet he did. He started a suit against the two dogs. As I recall, the case was settled out of court. Very embarrassing for one and all. How you dare bring this up, Charles Frederick Bush, I don't know.

We Move
to Houston

The elections in 1976 swept us Republicans out of office and Bar
and George raced for home—their home, not mine, in Houston,
Texas. George feels that when you're out, you should get out. We
bought a house in their old neighborhood, on another dead-end
street, and I had to work hard to make new dog friends. There were
three fenced-in German shepherds in the house behind us. They
were tremendous. They were also locked in, so I took many liberties
and called them terrible names. I flaunted the fact that I could
wander and roam at will and they couldn't. The only time in the four
years that we met with no brick wall separating us they had me
pinned in a second and were going for my throat when Bar threw
herself at them and they scampered away. I lay limp in Bar's arms
and she carried me upstairs and put me on our bed shaking and
sobbing wrapped in a blanket. I was faking, of course, and was found
out the minute the doorbell rang and I charged down the staircase
two steps at a time, to see who was there.

*Rin Tin Tin and Lassie move over. C. Fred could have won an Academy
Award for his performance.*

On the other side we had a tiny white poodle. We ignored each
other after a sniff or two. Farther down the street were two beautiful
golden retrievers. They were outdoor dogs and gently guarded
their house and greeted us all as we walked up and down the street.
A little farther up the street was an odd couple, a terrier with three
legs and a bouncing pinkish brown hunting dog, a puppy. His owner
adored him and refused to believe that he was gathering all the

neighborhood newspapers and hiding them. When the cache was found, all was forgiven and the pup was kept in until the papers were taken in.

All these dogs owned really wonderful people.

A little farther down the street in the bend of the road there was a house guarded by two cast-iron black labradors. I will confess that it took me months to wake up to the fact that they weren't alive and real. I barked at them every time we went by. I got braver and challenged them and still they didn't move. I darted forward and back and finally went right up to them and discovered they were statues. I just hope nobody saw me.

I quickly cased the neighborhood, marked our property lines off and settled in to enjoy civilian life. What I hadn't counted on was the addition to our family. Jeb and Columba Bush lived in Houston with their children, one-and-a-half-year-old George P. and new baby, Noelle. George and Bar adored these babies and the babies adored me. George P. walked like a drunken sailor in my direction every time he could and pulled my ears and tail. If I growled at the children George and Bar got furious, so I learned to lather them with kisses. They hated to be kissed and gave me a wide berth.

Brilliant, Freddy.

George took on many projects to feed us, which took him to Indiana, New Jersey, Texas and other places. He and Bar traveled a lot. They went back to China and saw all my old friends. They went to Tibet on this trip and were told that Bar was the third American woman to ever put her foot on Tibetan soil. During these years they also went to Hong Kong, Australia, Iran, Jordan, Singapore, Egypt, Israel, Greece and Denmark. These trips were for business and learning.

Good old Paula and Don had moved back to Houston with us. Don worked in a bank and lived way away from us. He bought a big blue pickup truck and took me for hours of riding. I loved standing on the spare-tire case in the back with the wind blowing my ears like flaps on a plane.

I was always sure he'd fly out.

Jeb and Columba moved to Caracas, Venezuela, for a year and Bar went to visit them. She missed them and the babies and, much to my surprise, so did I.

In 1977 the No. 1 Bush son, George W., who lived in West Texas, did two very exciting things. He announced for the United States Congress and he fell in love with and married Laura. He lost the congressional race, doggone it, but we all thought he was a big winner with Laura.

We went to Maine in the summers and looked across the bay at

Walker's Point. Ganny Bush's house was still there, but Uncle Herbie's house, "the big house," had been damaged severely by a storm in 1978 and nobody lived there. The house was for sale. It was so sad.

George announced on May 1, 1979, that he was going to run for the office of President of the United States of America. Everyone in the family went to Washington, D.C., for the announcement—everyone except me. I, of course, watched on TV. Everyone in the family worked in the campaign—everyone but me.

Jeb gave up his job at the bank in Venezuela and worked full-time as a volunteer. He traveled a lot and his family dog-sat for me. I loved to chase his kitten.

Jeb did tell me that he envisioned me baby-sitting with his children. He never thought he'd be sitting with my dog!

Neil, Marvin and Dorothy all left college and went to work for their father full-time. George W. worked part-time in West Texas. He was married, needed to get his business going and was quite frankly tired of politics after an eighteen-month race of his own. In spite of that he worked, and worked hard.

Bar says that campaigning was good for them all, that her children started treating her as an adult for the first time. She certainly learned how poised, grown-up and able they were. Campaigning was not good for me.

43

In the summer of 1979 George based the campaign out of the gray house in Maine. For six weeks he held seminars for three days and two nights in the middle of the week. I sat in on them all. Experts came from around the country—from universities, business and government—and discussed the economy, defense, agriculture, Social Security, foreign affairs, energy, etc., on successive weeks. They worked all day from nine to five with a break for lunch at our house. In the evening we'd have a clambake or a picnic on the rocks. All in all we had about forty-five different men and women up that summer and they stayed at friends' homes. It was a fascinating learning experience for us all.

The campaign seemed forever to me and I missed George and Bar.

I must say it did seem forever and we missed C. Fred also.

They had highs and lows, Iowa and Illinois, and on May 27 of 1980, with me present, George announced his withdrawal from the campaign in Houston, Texas. We went right off to Maine to get ready for Neil's wedding to Sharon, a girl he'd met in New Hampshire. You might say we won one and lost one in New Hampshire.

George decided to throw himself into civilian life debt-free, and so he took to the road again and went to the convention in Detroit totally out of debt, thanks to dear friends across the country who worked like people to raise the money still owed.

Neil and Sharon were married a week before the convention and went off to Europe on their honeymoon. George had assured them that he would not be the choice for Vice President. Bar and George promised me that they would return from the convention and we'd live happily ever after. I should have known better. My heart was broken when I saw George accept a golden retriever named Veep on television. I didn't know for three days that they gave him to a good friend.

We wouldn't do that to you, C. Fred.

It was decided that Washington should be our home during the general election. So back we moved to our nation's capital. We rented a tiny house on Lowell Street and once again I got to know new neighborhood dogs and cats. Amos and Andy came by to see me some and Paula and I held down the home front. Bar and George came home every Saturday night. The Secret Service moved in with us at this time and they joined the neighbors in trying to stop me from sleeping in the middle of the street. I chased raccoons. The raccoons came right up to the Secret Service and tried to take their midnight snacks out of their hands.

Big excitement came when a month before the election Marvin announced his engagement to Margaret with a June wedding in mind.

Bar and George, all their children, Ganny Bush, George's brother John and Don went to Texas for election night. Of course I watched on the tube with Paula in Washington. I was thrilled when they won because now I could really be with Amos—even though Amos teased me by asking, "How does it feel to belong to the Second Family?" I said right back, "Not bad when you remember they are second out of 225 million. Not bad, Am, not bad."

Vice President's House

January 20, 1981, started out like any other day. Bar fed me and let me out to check the Lowell Street neighborhood. It was a bright, sunny day. I noticed that there were mobs of people in the street at 7 A.M. Bar and George started having guests very early in the morning. George's mother, Ganny Bush, and George took coffee out to the motorcycle police and the members of the press. I loved visiting with so many people. Many neighbors came out to wave Bar and George off. Just before they left, Bar called me and I decided to go for a little walk. Everyone laughed. After a short chase I was put in the house. I really loved it when I read about my escapade in the Washington *Post* the next day.

Bar and George went to St. John's Church—The church of the presidents, where every President has prayed since Madison—for a prayer service with President-elect and Mrs. Reagan and all the family.

Don and Paula then left for the inauguration and I was left all alone to watch the ceremony on TV. Don says I probably saw more on TV than he and Paula did from the mall. I did see Amos's father, Justice Stewart, swear George in as the forty-third Vice President of the United States of America.

When Don and Paula returned they came with a group of people who put all of Bar's and George's clothes and boxes in a big van. I jumped in the van with them and we drove off. We went by two large white anchors and up to a large white victorian house on a hill. I took two trips in the van and when Paula stayed in the big white

51

house, I stayed. When Paula put down my dog bowl I knew we had moved again. That George just cannot keep a job. We have moved six times since I came to live with the Bushes. This house is by far the biggest.

Not really true—the house in China was bigger, but the grounds here are much bigger.

By 4:30 that afternoon all clothes were in place and 150 of our Bush-Pierce relatives started piling in. George saw his home for the next four years for the very first time filled with relatives. I saw the house before George. There was music, food, flowers and drinks, and I already felt at home. The transition of the government is a fascinating process. It took a lot of work by volunteers and staff, but we did it!

How right he is. I'm not sure what he *did—but many of the people who moved us in we didn't know and never saw. They were wonderful.*

I quickly explored and found out that the kitchen and laundry room are in the basement. The first floor has a dining room, a living room, a sun porch, a library with books about and by vice presidents —collected by Walter Mondale, forty-second Vice President of the United States of America—and a big entrance hall. On the second floor there are two big, beautiful bedrooms, a family sitting room and George's dressing room–office. George loves his little spot and works there every night with me by his feet and his pet bonefish on the wall. On the third floor there is one gymnasium-size bedroom and two tiny bedrooms where Paula reigns. I sleep there when George and Bar are gone. Bar has her office on the third floor. It's a combination office and exercise room with a stationary bike, a running machine, a typewriter, files and a desk. The walls are covered with pictures. There is one especially good one of me with President and Mrs. Reagan.

Everyone says, and it's true, that the Vice President's house has the best location in Washington. It is on ten acres of the United States Naval Observatory grounds. The grounds are covered with big, beautiful trees, lovely, well-tended plantings and has the best view in town. To the east we see the Capitol and the Washington Monument. That first evening after the family reception George, Bar and I climbed into our bed for a nap before the inaugural balls. Not the Rockefeller Max Ernst bed—it has long gone. The Rockefellers did leave some wonderful furniture. The dining room table, for instance, was in John D. Rockefeller's apartment in New York on West Fifty-fourth Street. It seats eighteen people.

We awakened to sparkling fireworks over the lighted city, our nation's capital. To the west we see the Washington Cathedral silhouetted on the top of Mount St. Albans. To the north of our house is the Naval Observatory, the atomic clock, the helicopter pad and the tennis court. I love to swim and there is *no* pool.

Too bad, Freddy.

Bar and George entertain a lot in this lovely old house, built in 1893. She has borrowed paintings from several museums. They are all painted by Americans—some primitives, many American Impressionists and some contemporary artists.

Many famous people have met me at these parties, but that's another chapter. At parties I put the hard press on guests for food. I have refined the ancient art of begging to a fine point. I get eye contact, I sit up, I sigh and if all else fails, I rest a paw on the guest's knee. This is plan A—I've never used plan B. Of course if Bar sees me the game is up.

On the whole I find parties boring and quickly ask to go outside and sit with my friends the uniform guards. I am an honorary member of the Secret Service Uniform Guard Division. Our house has five little guardhouses. I often change with whoever is on guard although my favorite post is No. 1 at the front gate. I love to greet George when he comes home by throwing myself yelping at the tires of his car. If I can bring the whole caravan to a halt, I am thrilled.

Being the Vice President's dog is not all biscuits and bones, you know.

Marvin and Margaret got married in June of 1981 in Richmond, Virginia, and I was not included. Of course, George P. and Noelle were there.

George and Bar are gone a lot. They have taken many foreign trips and travel around the United States a lot. I have grown to have a love-hate relationship with the helicopter. I love it when it brings them home and hate it when it takes them away. When the bags are brought out, I immediately sit around and sob and sulk.

He does and it almost ruins the start of every trip.

Thank heavens for Don. I love Don more than anyone in the world. He takes me for long walks every night he is in town. We look for raccoons and black squirrels that are unique to Washington. He knows when I am sick. He brings me presents and he takes me for long car rides with the windows wide open so my ears can blow in the wind.

As a surprise for Bar and George, Don took me to the White House and had an identification badge made for me. But George will not let me go to the office even with my own badge. (That's Don holding me for the picture.)

Don is a dog's best friend.

Every now and then I suspect George and I are dog-sitting Don's dog.

And thank heavens for Amos and Andy. They come and we walk Andy and Bar all around the observatory grounds every day they are in town together. They are getting older and no longer jog. Bad knees, *they* say.

What nerve, Amos is thirteen and you are ten, or in people language Amos is ninety-one and you are seventy.

Actually, we Bushes believe in lots of exercise. So I exercise Bar and George a lot. I jog with George. He says I'm lazy and he reports to Bar that I don't go all three miles. Does he think I'm dumb? Why go around in circles when I can wait and he'll come back to me?

I have more trouble exercising Bar. I take Bar out once a day and let her hit tennis balls to me. I pretend I don't see where she hits them and look every which way—shaking my head and tail and looking back toward her. So, of course, Bar retrieves the ball. I very

often bring the ball halfway back and then roll on it or sit on it. She has to come to me: more exercise for Bar. When I'm through playing I take my ball and go up on the porch. The game's over. Remember, I am seventy.

I sneaked out one night while Bar was gone and George found me at 5 A.M. with my ear caught on a fence. I was calling on the admiral's lady dog and not only did not get into her yard, I could not return home. It was humiliating.

I was further unsettled several months later when a national sporting magazine ran a picture of George and Bar and me. The photo caption identified me as a golden retriever. However, I was considerably mollified soon thereafter when the magazine's editors sent me my own personal backpack.

I have been in magazines and newspapers many times. The pictures show me with George on the boat, me with George on the wall in Maine and me with George jogging. I've heard people say, "Who's that man with C. Fred Bush?" Immediately after the inauguration the following appeared in several weekly papers:

Of course you know who won the contest—there's nothing secret from the Secret Service.

The volume of my mail picked up and I have several pen pals. One letter came from an admirer after she had seen my pictures in a national magazine.

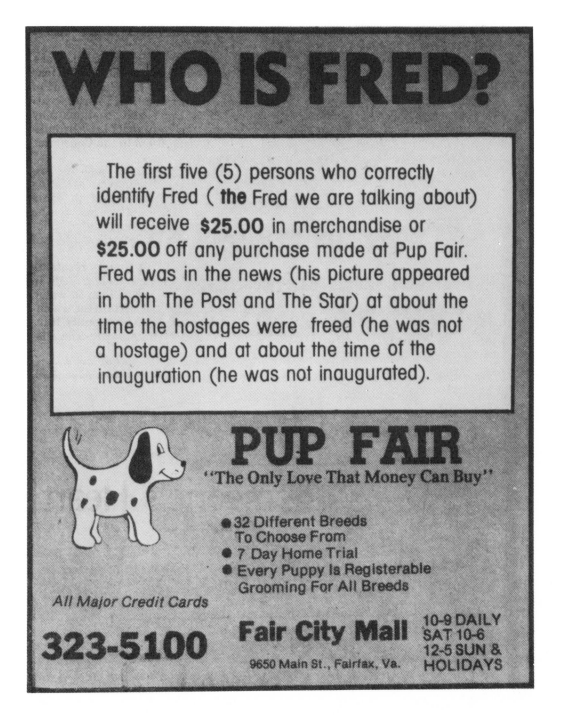

My admirer ended by saying, "I hope, C. Fred, your master will permit us to meet." I couldn't resist and wrote back: "Where do you get that 'master' from? Look at the picture again, please. Who's opening the door for whom?"

The article was supposed to be about George. C. Fred was in three of the four pictures. The fourth picture was of the house. George was in two of the four pictures.

I often get letters asking me what I like to eat—do I get scraps from the table? I have been on a diet since the day I arrived. For ten years Bar has fed me half a can of diet dog food every morning and the other half every night. I like table scraps very much—but she won't let anyone feed me. George slips me a snack under the table when she is not looking.

Bar and George, on the other hand, eat all the time—wonderful, rich, varied food.

Are you kidding? Who gets rich food on the rubber chicken circuit?

Bar says she wished she remembered her son George W. before dinner instead of after dinner. He always says, "Go on, Mom, eat it today . . . and wear it tomorrow." I still wish I wasn't on a diet and could eat table scraps!

I had several proposals of marriage through the mail. Believe it or not, George liked one letter so much that he answered and accepted one on my behalf. Can you imagine if the shoe had been on the other foot? But that's the next chapter.

This may be an appropriate time to say that I am getting tired of answering mail for a dog.

Marriage

In the summer of 1977 George and Bar were living in Houston. I was four years old. A marriage was arranged for me without one person even asking me. I never had a more miserable three days. She was a pretty little thing, blond, very much a liberated woman. And very aggressive. This little hussy was brought to our house. We had a fenced-in backyard with a swimming pool. The whole back of our house was glass. I, who was always free to wander in and out, was suddenly locked out with this wild female. Early on I discovered that she didn't swim, so I took seventeen swims on that first day alone. I scratched on the glass doors and windows on every side. I tried for eye contact with just anybody who walked by. It was all to no avail. I finally learned that I could climb up on the terrace table and she couldn't. She was picked up each evening and returned in the morning for yet another agonizing day.

Freddy is right. They were agonizing days and we just hated it for him. The next time C. Fred got married, he went to the veterinarian for the marriage rites.

Same female, same results. I really didn't like her at all.

All the blame was put on C. Fred for the lack of success of this marriage. There was much talk of his failure—spread, we're sure, by the rejected lady, a woman scorned, etc.

After we moved back to Washington to the Vice President's house my life took on a certain glamour and my picture started appearing regularly in the papers and magazines. Bar started getting letters written to me. Some were from dog lovers and many were from female dog owners urging another marriage. There was even a proposal from an Argentinian dog. Bar put her foot down. She said, "No foreign affairs for Fred." One letter came from Buffy Chiles, whose owner had seen my picture in George's press office. Buffy's letter had a flair to it. It was catchy and ended "And so, dear Fred, if you agree, your place or mine?" The marriage was arranged and we were married on the tenth of May 1982.

In the middle of July we got the word that Buffy and I had had seven children, six girls and one boy. Bar and Don went over to see the pups. She told me later that on the wall, over the nest, was my picture with DAD written under it.

It was there that Bar learned what it was about Buff that I liked. Buffy was a redhead.

I was surprised at first, for I had hoped for a blond male puppy and the only blondes were girls. Wouldn't you think with a name like "Buffy" we were talking about a blond, honey-colored, buff-colored, yellow dog? Buffy is smaller than C. Fred and has a wonderful topknot of blond hair. The rest is red. She is an English cocker, a good little mother, and I grew to respect and love her. Now that I think about it—the admiral's dog was a setter, a redhead.

There was much talk about my son joining us in Maine at the end of August. By this time George had sold the gray house and bought part of Walker's Point. I thought he wanted a place for me to run and play and swim, but not at all—he wanted to be near his mother and have a place for *all* the grandchildren, he said. *All* the grandchildren? How many more? Bar had already overloaded the circuit with Laura and George's twins, Jenna and Barbara, ten-month-old crawlers (who seemed to delight Bar and George), and George P. and Noelle, now six and five. She and George seemed to forget me. She constantly was pushing me out of the room and out of the house. Dorothy and Bill LeBlond got married on September 1 and I was just always in the way. So the pup was given to dear friends—in my opinion a very appropriate move on the Bushes' part—who named him G. Walker, a very appropriate name. As it is, there is barely room on our bed for the three of us!

Several times in the fall G. Walker called on us. At first he appealed to me. He was a gangly redhead with wonderful blond eyebrows and blond curls on the top of his little red head. I found him slightly amusing as he jumped over my head, under my legs and skidded on the fallen fall leaves. I was always truly relieved when he jumped back into his car and drove home.

G. Walker called on us for one last time in March when G.W. was eight months old. Suddenly I felt old—he is as big as I am and full of pep. We had two rather unpleasant skirmishes and, thank heavens, Bar and George agreed with me that I am an "only" dog and not very paternal at that.

Famous People Who Know C. Fred Bush

Name-dropping comes naturally for the Bushes—it's almost a competitive sport. You never say, "I know so and so." You always say, "So and so knows me." Here are a few folks who know me:

Happy Rockefeller

Charlton Heston

His Excellency Jorge Antonio Aja Espil, Ambassador of Argentina

General Carlos Romulo

Israeli Prime Minister Shamir

Prince and Princess Sadruddin Aga Khan

Prime Minister Margaret Thatcher of England

Crown Prince Hassan ibn Talal of Jordan

Prince Claus and Queen Beatrix

Christopher Reeve

Gene Hackman

John Newcombe

King Hassan of Morocco

Astronauts John Young and Robert Crippen

Epilogue

As a wrap-up to C. Fred's story—a story that I hope will go on for a long, long time—I would say that only another dog lover could ever understand the great pleasure this loyal, loving little fellow has given to us.

I took C. Fred in for his yearly rabies shot recently and when the girl handed me the receipt, I noticed that she'd put him down as a ten-year-old male golden cocker. And so Freddy, that buff, blond, honey-colored, gray-and-yellow dog, has finally found his true color—gold.